P9-CBF-445

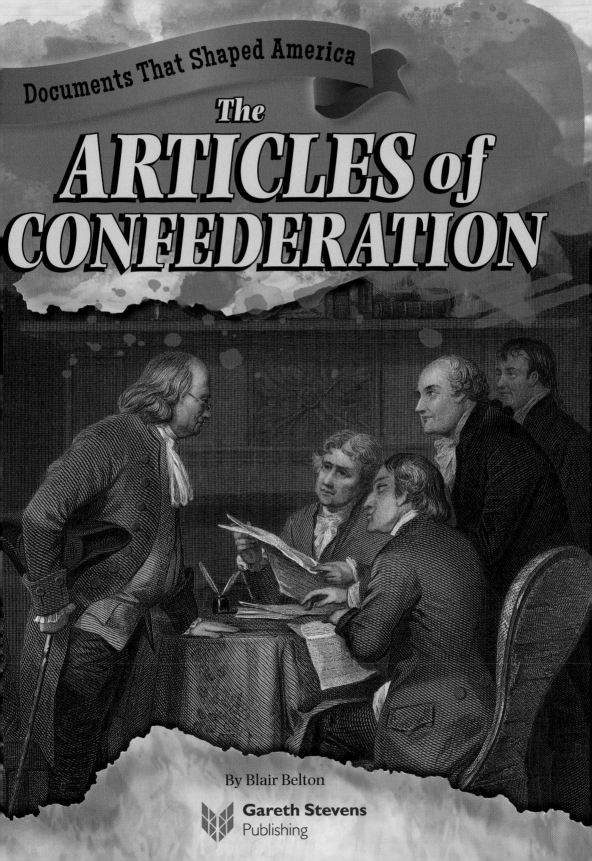

Documents That Shaped America

The
ARTICLES of
CONFEDERATION

By Blair Belton

Gareth Stevens
Publishing

Please visit our website, www.garethstevens.com. For a free color catalog of all our high-quality books, call toll free 1-800-542-2595 or fax 1-877-542-2596.

Library of Congress Cataloging-in-Publication Data

Belton, Blair.
The Articles of Confederation / by Blair Belton.
  p. cm. — (Documents that shaped America)
Includes index.
ISBN 978-1-4339-8994-0 (pbk.)
ISBN 978-1-4339-8995-7 (6-pack)
ISBN 978-1-4339-8993-3 (library binding)
1. United States. — Articles of Confederation — Juvenile literature. 2. Constitutional history — United States – Juvenile literature. 3. United States — Politics and government — 1775-1783 — Juvenile literature. I. Title.
KF4508.B45 2014
342.7302—d23

First Edition

Published in 2014 by
Gareth Stevens Publishing
111 East 14th Street, Suite 349
New York, NY 10003

Designer: Sarah Liddell
Editor: Therese Shea

Photo credits: Cover, pp. 1, 8 Stock Montage/Contributor/Archive Photos/Getty Images; p. 5 John Parrot/Stocktrek Images/Getty Images; p. 7 photo courtesy of Wikimedia Commons, Congress voting independence.jpg; p. 9 MPI/Stringer/Archive Photos/ Getty Images; p. 11 (charter) photo courtesy of Wikimedia Commons, Carolina Charter 1663.jpg; p. 11 (constitution) photo courtesy of Wikimedia Commons, VtConstitution.png; p. 13 photo courtesy of Wikimedia Commons, John Dickinson portrait.jpg; p. 15 amorfati.art/Shutterstock.com; p. 16 Hulton Archive/Stringer/Hulton Archive/ Getty Images; pp. 17, 19 DEA PICTURE LIBRARY/Contributor/De Agostini/ Getty Images; p. 21 (Franklin) Herbert Orth/Contributor/TIME & LIFE Images/ Getty Images; p. 21 (articles) photo courtesy of Wikimedia Commons, Articles page1.jpg; p. 22 photo courtesy of Wikimedia Commons, PreliminaryTreatyOfParisPainting.jpg; p. 23 photo courtesy of Wikimedia Commons, TreatOfParisDraftLastPage.jpg; p. 24 UniversalImagesGroup/Contributor/Universal Images Group/Getty Images; p. 25 photo courtesy of Wikimedia Commons, Articles page5.jpg; p. 27 (one third dollar) photo courtesy of Wikimedia Commons, Continental Currency One-Third-Dollar 17-Feb-76 obv.jpg; p. 27 (fifty-five dollar) photo courtesy of Wikimedia Commons, Benjamin Franklin nature printed 55 dollar from 1779.jpg; p. 27 (three pence note) photo courtesy of Wikimedia Commons, Pennsylvania three pence note front.jpg; p. 28 photo courtesy of Wikimedia Commons, Unidentified Artist - Daniel Shays and Job Shattuck - Google Art Project.jpg.

Printed in the United States of America

CPSIA compliance information: Batch #CS13GS: For further information contact Gareth Stevens, New York, New York at 1-800-542-2595.

CONTENTS

Words in the glossary appear in **bold** type the first time they are used in the text.

A NEW COUNTRY

On July 4, 1776, delegates from the American colonies approved the Declaration of Independence. The **document** asserted the "thirteen united States of America" were free from England's power. But if the Americans weren't ruled by the British king, who would rule them? The delegates who were meeting in Philadelphia, Pennsylvania, as the Second Continental Congress were a temporary organization. One of their tasks was to define a new and permanent government for the American states in a **constitution**.

The delegates faced many obstacles: The colonies had different religions, economies, views on slavery, and little practice working together. Nonetheless, they needed to band together against England, the most powerful country in the world. They had to find common ground in their shared beliefs of a just government.

It's a Fact!

The rattlesnake became a popular image for colonists who wanted independence from England. The snake represented a willingness to defend oneself with a dangerous bite.

JOIN, or DIE.

COLONIAL COOPERATION

The American colonists were accustomed to taking orders from the royal government in England, but they weren't used to taking orders from other colonies. They viewed a central government with suspicion. The American colonies had cooperated just a few times in the past, including protecting themselves from invasions. But other than the threat of foreign attacks and conflicts with Native Americans, there had been little reason to work together.

DIFFICULTIES and DIVISIONS

In 1776, the Second Continental Congress dealt with the difficulty of creating the right government for the states. Americans didn't want another government that would tax them, limit their movement into western lands, or make them practice a religion. Many worried about a government that would abolish slavery, while others feared slavery's continuation. However, Americans did want a government that could protect them from hostile Native Americans and foreign nations and, more immediately, win the American Revolution.

As the delegates began their discussions, it became clear that if the states were to agree to a new central government, each would have to give up some independence. Talk of states giving power to a central government proved to be divisive.

It's a Fact!

In 1763, the British tried to prevent wars with Native American tribes by keeping colonists from moving west.

ONE COUNTRY OR THIRTEEN?

Many American colonists had great love for their home colony. When General George Washington asked New Jersey troops to swear loyalty to the United States of America, the soldiers replied, "New Jersey is our country." Some people even disliked other colonies. The will of Lewis Morris of New York said that his son, Gouverneur Morris, could be educated any place except Connecticut because of "that low craft and cunning so incident in the people of that country."

Delegates to the Second Continental Congress, as well as the people they represented, followed different religious traditions. For example, Connecticut and other New England states favored the Congregational Church. Pennsylvania had many Quakers, and the southern states followed the Church of England. Members of these religions hadn't always gotten along peacefully.

Slavery was an even more conflict-ridden issue. It seemed critical to the southern plantation economy, but many in the North wanted it to end. Abigail Adams wrote to her husband, John Adams, in 1774: "I wish most sincerely there was not a slave in this province. It always appeared a most **iniquitous** scheme to me—to fight ourselves for what we are daily robbing and plundering from those who have as good a right to freedom as we have."

Abigail Adams

It's a Fact!

In the 1650s, Massachusetts declared any Quaker speaking out could have their ears cut off, an iron spike driven through their tongue, or be hung. Religion was a source of many bloody colonial conflicts.

Despite differing views of
slavery and religion, the members
of the Second Continental
Congress managed to agree on a
constitution eventually.

AM I NOT A MAN AND A BROTHER?

A COOPERATIVE CONGRESS

In 1774, at the initial meeting of the First Continental Congress,
the first subject of **debate** was who should lead the meeting with
a prayer. John Jay of New York and John Rutledge of South Carolina
thought that no minister of one religion would be acceptable to all
since they practiced different religions. Congregationalist Samuel
Adams of Massachusetts wanted to establish trust among the
delegates, so he asked a Church of England minister to lead
the prayer.

GOVERNING LAWS

The delegates to the Second Continental Congress were chosen from their colonial legislatures and had some common views of how government operated. Each colony had been governed under a type of **charter**, with a royally appointed governor and a legislature elected by the colonists or chosen by the king. The delegates were familiar with how charters had provided certain limits on royal powers.

Each colony created state constitutions to replace their British charter. Two—New Hampshire and South Carolina—did this before the Declaration of Independence! New York was the last to finish its constitution in 1777. So the delegates to the Second Continental Congress had already heard many debates and discussions about what should be in a governing document.

It's a Fact!

Some constitutions aren't written in a single document. The British constitution is a collection of laws and traditions.

The Vermont state constitution was the first to abolish slavery.

state constitution

COLONIAL CHARTERS

Colonial charters were documents that granted land in North America to businesses, groups of people, or individuals. Charters provided legal proof of ownership, defined the rights of settlers in those lands, and outlined the form and function of governments. Some state constitutions used ideas found in their original charters. Similarly, the delegates to the Second Continental Congress looked to the state constitutions when writing a constitution for their new country.

colonial charter

The DICKINSON DRAFT

On June 12, 1776, the Second Continental Congress appointed a committee consisting of one delegate from each colony to draft a constitution. John Dickinson of Pennsylvania led the committee, and the first draft is often called the Dickinson draft.

This document proposed a strong central government with the right to override state laws. The government would have a Congress in which each state got one vote. This Congress could settle disputes between states, control western settlement, declare war and make peace, and conduct affairs with foreign nations. The states would keep **militias** ready in case of conflict, but Congress would appoint officers. This government wouldn't be able to impose taxes. Instead, each state would contribute to the national treasury based on its population. The Second Continental Congress began debating points in the Dickinson draft in July 1776.

It's a Fact!

John Dickinson had opposed the Declaration of Independence because he feared that the colonies wouldn't be able to work together. He refused to sign it.

John Dickinson headed the committee that wrote the first draft of the Articles of **Confederation**.

John Dickinson

WHY WEAK?

Many delegates of the Second Continental Congress believed a weak government strengthened their rights as individual citizens. As British colonists, they had suffered under powerful royal governors and officials. Though colonies had legislatures, decisions could be and had been controlled by British officials appointed by the king. From this experience, most delegates didn't want a king or governing officials who could act against the demands of the people.

DEBATING the DRAFT

The delegates couldn't agree on a new constitution for over a year because of the ongoing war and several issues in the Dickinson draft:

- <u>One state, one vote</u>: The states with many people wanted more than one vote in the new Congress. Small states thought each state should have one vote.
- <u>State contributions to the national treasury</u>: States with few slaves thought everyone should be counted towards the contribution of funds. States with many slaves didn't want the money they owed to the treasury to be based on their slave population.
- <u>Western lands</u>: States with claims to western lands didn't want to surrender those valuable properties to the central government.
- <u>Power of central government</u>: Many thought the Dickinson draft allowed the central government too much control over the states.

It's a Fact!

Virginia had claims that included everything west of the Ohio River to the Mississippi River. This was known as the Northwest Territory.

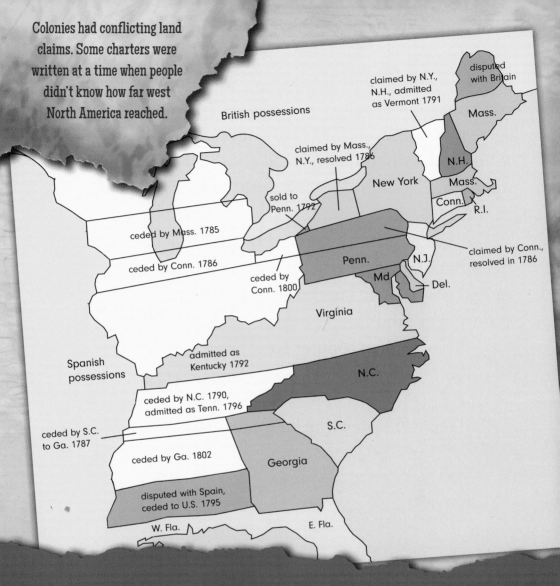

Colonies had conflicting land claims. Some charters were written at a time when people didn't know how far west North America reached.

British possessions

claimed by N.Y., N.H., admitted as Vermont 1791

disputed with Britain

Mass.

claimed by Mass., N.Y., resolved 1786

N.H.

New York

Mass.

sold to Penn. 1792

Conn.

R.I.

ceded by Mass. 1785

ceded by Conn. 1786

claimed by Conn., resolved in 1786

ceded by Conn. 1800

Penn.

N.J.

Md

Del.

Virginia

Spanish possessions

admitted as Kentucky 1792

N.C.

ceded by N.C. 1790, admitted as Tenn. 1796

ceded by S.C. to Ga. 1787

S.C.

ceded by Ga. 1802

Georgia

disputed with Spain, ceded to U.S. 1795

W. Fla.

E. Fla.

WESTERN LANDS

Massachusetts, New York, Connecticut, Virginia, North Carolina, South Carolina, and Georgia had colonial charters that extended their land westward, to the Mississippi River or even to the Pacific Ocean. With British limits on westward movement removed, the territory would be available for settlement. The lands of the Ohio River valley would be worth a great deal of money to landowners and settlers, too. States wanted to profit from these properties.

In April 1777, North Carolina delegate Thomas Burke led the charge to strip the Dickinson draft's central government of power over the states. Most delegates agreed with him, so the document was amended. New wording promised states would retain all "**sovereignty**, rights, and freedoms," except those specifically granted to the new Congress.

The delegates decided to keep the Dickinson draft's rule of one vote for each state. They also dropped the central government's authority to set boundaries for states and western lands.

John Witherspoon of New Jersey suggested that the contribution of each state should be based on the value of its land instead of its population. This idea was adopted as well, though the New England states voted in opposition.

John Witherspoon

It's a Fact!

When the French allied with the Americans, they didn't just battle the British in America, but in India, South Africa, and other places around the world.

The surrender of British general
John Burgoyne at Saratoga,
New York, convinced France that
the American soldiers would be
worthy allies.

The surrender of British general John Burgoyne at Saratoga, New York, convinced France that the American soldiers would be worthy allies.

THE TURNING POINT OF THE WAR

On October 17, 1777, the Americans forced the British army to surrender at Saratoga, New York. The battle proved that American soldiers weren't doomed to lose the war. France became interested in becoming an American **ally**, which they formally announced in 1778. The Americans knew a united government was important to receive support from foreign nations. The Second Continental Congress moved ahead with compromises to create a permanent government.

17

RATIFICATION

On November 15, 1777, the Second Continental Congress agreed on a new constitution called the Articles of Confederation. After sending it out to the states and making corrections, the delegates signed the Articles on July 9, 1778. Next, all 13 states had to formally approve, or ratify, the document.

Legislatures of 10 states ratified the new constitution quickly. Small states had complaints about western land issues. Maryland, in particular, was stubborn. It wanted larger states to give up, or cede, their western territory to the national government. On January 2, 1781, Virginia offered to cede land claims north and west of the Ohio River. Maryland finally ratified the Articles on March 1, 1781. With that, the Articles of Confederation became the first constitution of the United States of America.

It's a Fact!

The word "congress" is from a Latin word meaning "to come together." Congress became the official name of the US national legislature.

The French and British navies battle in the Chesapeake Bay near Maryland in 1782.

UNDER PRESSURE

Virginia giving up its western claims wasn't the only event that made Maryland ratify the Articles of Confederation. In 1780, the British navy began attacking Maryland towns along the Chesapeake Bay. Maryland officials asked the French ambassador for the protection of the French navy. The ambassador suggested that his country's navy would be more likely to aid the state if it ratified the Articles. Ratification came immediately.

The 13 ARTICLES

An article is a piece of writing, and the Articles of Confederation were made up of 13 articles:

Article I formally named the new nation, declaring "The Stile of this confederacy shall be, 'The United States of America.' "

Article II promised each state would retain its independence and "every Power, **Jurisdiction** and right," except those given to the central government.

Article III stated the purpose of the United States was a "league of friendship" to assist each other in defending themselves against outside attacks and in promoting their shared interests.

Article IV allowed residents of each state to travel to other states where they would be given "all privileges" of free inhabitants. Runaway criminals would be taken back to the state of the crime.

It's a Fact!

Benjamin Franklin outlined a constitution in 1775 even before the Americans had declared independence from England.

Benjamin Franklin had sought an alliance of the American colonies since 1754.

To all to whom

THE CONGRESS OF THE CONFEDERATION

Article V said that the new Congress would be made up of two to seven delegates from each state, and these "delegates shall be annually appointed in such manner as the legislature of each state shall direct." Each state would have just one vote in Congress. Delegates would serve no more than 3 years in a 6-year period. To protect freedom of speech, they were protected from arrest while serving in Congress except in certain cases.

Benjamin Franklin

Article VI said states couldn't engage in foreign affairs, declare war, or maintain an army without the approval of Congress. However, every state was required to "keep up a well regulated and disciplined militia."

Article VII declared that if armed forces were needed, states would name "all officers of or under the rank of colonel" to lead armed forces from that state.

Article VIII explained the central government paid for defense using a treasury, which would be "supplied by the several states, in proportion to the value of all land within each state."

Article IX listed powers of the central government, called "the united States, in congress assembled," including: declaring war, making treaties, dealing with foreign countries, and settling disputes between states. Almost all major decisions required nine votes in Congress.

It's a Fact!

The American Revolution ended with the Treaty of Paris in 1783. Congress had so little money that by 1785 all US navy ships were sold off.

full Powers, signed with our Hands the
Treaty, and caused the Seals of our Arms

Done at Paris, this the
In the Year of our Lord, one thousand   hundred
and Eighty three. —

B Hartley

John. Adams..

B Franklin

John Jay

MILITIAS

In 1777, people viewed a standing army, or one that operates
even in peacetime, with suspicion. Americans had felt threatened
by the standing army of the British forces. Soldiers were always
present and sometimes demanded food and shelter. Congress
intended the states to have militias for temporary and
emergency use. Although the central government had the power
to maintain an army and navy, they could only do so with each
state's cooperation.

Article X gave the powers of Congress to a "committee of the states" when Congress wasn't in session.

Article XI allowed for Canada to join the United States, as well as future colonies "if agreed to by nine states." (Many Americans thought the British Canadian colonies would join them in seeking independence.)

Article XII promised the new nation would take over all debts and "monies borrowed" by the Congress during the American Revolution.

Article XIII said all states should obey the decisions of Congress and follow the Articles of Confederation. The union of the states was "**perpetual**," and no changes would be allowed to the Articles of Confederation unless Congress and all states agreed.

It's a Fact!

A "committee of states" was only used once, in the summer of 1784. So few delegates showed up that nothing got done.

None of the Articles of Confederation dealt with the divisive issues of slavery or religion. If they had been included, it's possible the Articles would never have been ratified.

TROUBLE TO COME

Article XIII hinted at the shortcomings of the central government under the Articles of Confederation. Article XIII doesn't give the government any powers over states disobeying the Articles. For example, if states failed to send delegates to Congress, there were no consequences. It later seemed the states were eager to work together to defend themselves against the British, but when that threat was gone, they easily ignored much of the Articles of Confederation.

WEAKNESSES

A major problem facing the new government was money. Though each state was required to contribute to the treasury, there were no drawbacks to not paying. States were dealing with their own debts, and, in fact, Georgia and North Carolina paid nothing to the central treasury. Attempts to change the Articles and give Congress the power to tax goods in order to raise money failed.

The only way to obtain funds for the nation's debts and expenses was to print more money, and this caused merchants to raise prices. The American army suffered from a lack of supplies during the war. George Washington complained to Congress: "a wagon full of money will scarcely purchase a wagon load of provisions." Sometimes businesses wouldn't even take government money.

It's a Fact!

The 1783 Treaty of Paris required the American government to pay people who had been loyal to England for property taken during the war. The penniless Congress couldn't make these payments, so the British kept forts in American territory.

The lack of a stable money source meant that many people couldn't repay their debts. States made their own money, further confusing the problem.

NORTHWEST ORDINANCE

One achievement of the Congress of the Confederation was the Northwest **Ordinance**. This legislation, passed on July 13, 1787, allowed for settlement of the Northwest Territory. The territory was officially acquired from England under the Treaty of Paris at the end of the American Revolution in 1783. The Northwest Ordinance outlined the government of the territory, described how states could be made from it, and even forbade slavery within its borders.

Other problems under the Articles of Confederation in the new country became evident as time went on. In Massachusetts, Daniel Shays and 2,000 farmers rose up in anger against the state government in 1786. They couldn't pay rising property taxes and were faced with the threat of losing their land. Although the **rebellion** was put down in 1787, many feared it was just the beginning of similar conflicts.

Calls began for a stronger central government. A Constitutional Convention was assembled in Philadelphia in May 1787. There, rather than amending the Articles, the delegates wrote a new constitution. It was ratified in 1789. The Articles of Confederation, the first constitution of the United States, became a piece of the young country's past.

It's a Fact!

The public debt acquired by the United States under the Articles of Confederation was more than $75 million.

News of Shays' Rebellion convinced many people of the need for a stronger central government that could maintain order.

TIMELINE OF THE ARTICLES OF CONFEDERATION

1776
Committee appointed to write Articles of Confederation

1777
Battle of Saratoga

1778
Congress signs final draft of Articles of Confederation

1781
Articles of Confederation ratified

1783
Treaty of Paris ends American Revolution

1786
Annapolis Convention

1787
Constitutional Convention begins

1789
US Constitution ratified

OYSTERS AND A NEW CONSTITUTION

Maryland and Virginia had fought for many years over the right to collect oysters in the Potomac River. This ongoing conflict showed what little power the Confederation Congress had over interstate problems. A meeting in Annapolis, Maryland, in 1786 was set to make decisions about regulating trade between states. When too few delegates showed up from the invited states, the Annapolis Convention sent out a call for the Constitutional Convention.

29

GLOSSARY

ally: one of two or more people, groups, or countries who work together

charter: an official agreement giving permission to do something

confederation: a league of people or states that support each other and act together

constitution: the basic laws by which a country or state is governed

debate: an argument or public discussion

document: a formal piece of writing

iniquitous: wicked or acting with great injustice

jurisdiction: the authority to enforce laws

militia: a group of citizens who organize like soldiers in order to protect themselves

ordinance: a law or rule

perpetual: lasting forever

rebellion: a fight to overthrow a government

sovereignty: the right to self-government

FOR MORE INFORMATION

BOOKS

Rebman, Renée C. *The Articles of Confederation*. Minneapolis, MN: Compass Point Books, 2006.

Sonneborn, Liz. *The Articles of Confederation*. Chicago, IL: Heinemann Library, 2013.

Waxman, Laura Hamilton. *What Are the Articles of Confederation? And Other Questions About the Birth of the United States*. Minneapolis, MN: Lerner Publications Company, 2012.

WEBSITES

American Revolution
*www.havefunwithhistory.com/HistorySubjects/
AmericanRevolution.html*
Check out links to short videos and other resources about the American Revolution.

Articles of Confederation
www.ourdocuments.gov/doc.php?flash=true&doc=3
See images of the original document.

The Articles of Confederation
bensguide.gpo.gov/6-8/documents/articles/index.html
This is a summary of the Articles of Confederation.

INDEX